curious about
CATS

BY M. K. OSBORNE

AMICUS · AMICUS INK

What are you

curious about?

CHAPTER **3** THREE

Cat Training

PAGE

16

Curious About is published
by Amicus and Amicus Ink
P.O. Box 227
Mankato, MN 56002
www.amicuspublishing.us

Editor: Alissa Thielges
Series Designer: Kathleen Petelinsek
Book Designer: Ciara Beitlich
Photo researcher: Bridget Prehn

Library of Congress Cataloging-in-Publication Data
Names: Osborne, M. K., author.
Title: Curious about cats / by M. K. Osborne
Description: Mankato, MN : Amicus, [2021] | Series:
Curious about pets | Includes bibliographical references and
index. | Audience: Ages 6–9 | Audience: Grades 2–3
Identifiers: LCCN 2019053800 (print) | LCCN 2019053801
(ebook) | ISBN 9781681519654 (library binding) | ISBN
9781681526126 (paperback) | ISBN 9781645490500 (pdf)
Subjects: LCSH: Cats—Juvenile literature.
Classification: LCC SF445.7 .K64 2021 (print) |
LCC SF445.7 (ebook) | DDC 636.8—dc23
LC record available at https://lccn.loc.gov/2019053800
LC ebook record available at https://lccn.loc.gov/2019053801

Photos © iStock/drbimages cover, 1; iStock/undefined undefined
2 (left), 6; Shutterstock/Nils Jacobi 2 (right), 11 (top); Shutterstock/
Kristi Blokhin 3, 17; iStock/vvvita 5; iStock/CBCK-Christine 7;
Shutterstock/Tanakorn Thongkittidilok 8–9; Dreamstime/Makarova
Olga 11 (icons); Shutterstock/hayata kummok 12; Shutterstock/
Nils Jacobi 13; iStock/Dixi_ 14–15; GmbH 18; Shutterstock/
noreefly 19; Alamy/Kevin Wells 20; Shutterstock/Eric Isselee 21
(Ragdoll), Tony Campbell 21 (Siamese), PHOTOCREO Michal
Bednarek 21 (British shorthair), Jagodka 21 (Persian), Kucher Serhii
21 (Maine coon)

CHAPTER ONE

Why do cats rub up against things?

Cats like to mark things with their scent. It makes them feel safe. They do this by rubbing their body against it. All cat **breeds** do this. Has a cat rubbed against you? It likes you! A cat may even rub her head on you. This is called **bunting**.

Cats mark things they consider
theirs—even humans.

Why does my cat put its butt in my face?

This may seem weird, but your cat is being friendly. Humans shake hands or hug. Cats rub against people to say hello. The base of a cat's tail has scent **glands**. When you pet her there, you pick up her scent. You are also leaving your scent on her.

Cats rub their scent on things around their home, too.

CHAPTER TWO

My cat is always sleeping. Is it lazy?

Probably not. Cats sleep a lot. Some rest up to 20 hours a day! But they don't always fall asleep. Their eyes may be open slightly. Their ears and whiskers may twitch. They still know what is going on around them. Wild cats do this, too. They save energy to hunt later.

DID YOU KNOW?
Cats can dream when they are in a deep sleep.

How do cats land on their feet when they fall?

Cats have an incredible sense of balance. They can always tell which way is up. As a cat falls, it bends its spine. It pulls its legs in. This helps it twist in the air. Then its feet spread to land softly. This all takes less than one second!

A cat keeps an eye on where it will land.

Head turns

DID YOU KNOW?
Cats have a flexible spine.
This helps them twist
when falling.

Feet spread to land

Spine rotates

Legs line up

Why does my cat run around at night?

Cats aren't afraid of the dark—they can see at night.

Cats are **nocturnal**. They are most active at night. In the wild, this is when they hunt. Their eyes see well in the dark. Their whiskers are like extra fingers. They can sense and feel. They help a cat move around without bumping into things.

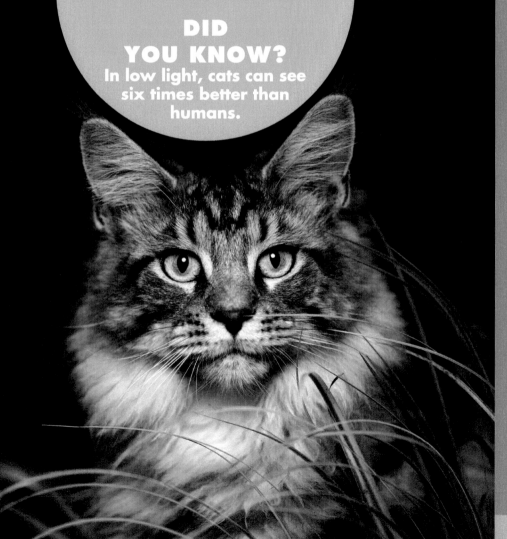

DID YOU KNOW?
In low light, cats can see six times better than humans.

Why does my cat sometimes bite when I pet it?

This cat feels comfortable
showing its belly.

Like you, cats sometimes don't want to be touched. Or they only want a quick pet. Most cats don't like belly rubs. The belly is a **vulnerable** area. Petting that area can upset a cat. A cat who shows its belly trusts you.

CAN I PET HERE?

EHHH MAYBE

YES!

AWESOME

PURRFECT

NAH

NOPE

BETTER NOT

NAH UH

STOP

Can I teach my cat tricks?

Of course! Cats are just as smart as dogs. But they can be harder to train. Cats are **stubborn**. They hear you talking to them. They just don't always care. You can get their interest with treats. Reward the behavior you want to see.

It takes a lot of practice
to teach a cat a trick.

A scratching post may stop your cat from shredding your furniture.

How can I stop my cat from scratching my things?

DID YOU KNOW?
A cat's claws are like
its fingertips. They help
a cat climb, walk,
and balance.

Cats scratch for many reasons. It sharpens their claws. It stretches their muscles. It marks their space. And it is fun to do. It is not so fun when they scratch your couch, though. To stop this, give your cat a scratching post. Reward them for using it. Then cover the couch with sticky tape. Cats don't like how that feels.

Can I take my cat for a walk?

A harness and leash keep a cat safe outside.

Yes! You can teach your cat to walk on a leash. A trip outside can be good for a cat. It is a new place to explore. But some cats may not like it. There are lots of new sights and smells. They get scared. That's okay. Watching from a window is fun for a cat, too!

RAGDOLL

SIAMESE

BRITISH SHORTHAIR

PERSIAN

MAINE COON

ASK MORE QUESTIONS

I want a pet cat. What breed would be best for me?

🐾

How did wild cats become pets?

🐾

Try a BIG QUESTION: How do cats help people?

SEARCH FOR ANSWERS

Search the library catalog or the Internet.
A librarian, teacher, or parent can help you.

Using Keywords
Find the looking glass.

🔍

Keywords are the most important words in your question.

❓

If you want to know about:

- different cat breeds, type: CAT BREEDS

- how wild cats became pets, type: CAT DOMESTICATION

FIND GOOD SOURCES

Here are some good, safe sources you can use in your research.
An adult can help you find more.

Books

Cats: Questions and Answers
by Christina Gardeski, 2017.

Is a Cat a Good Pet for Me?
by Theresa Emminizer, 2020.

Internet Sites

Ask Smithsonian: Have Cats Been Domesticated?
https://www.smithsonianmag.com/
smithsonian-institution/ask-smithsonian-are-
cats-domesticated-180955111/
The Smithsonian is a national museum and research center. It shares new discoveries in science, history, art, and technology.

The Cat Fanciers' Association: Cat Breeds
http://www.cfa.org/breeds
The CFA is a national cat organization. It is a great source for cat information.

Every effort has been made to ensure that these websites are appropriate for children. However, because of the nature of the Internet, it is impossible to guarantee that these sites will remain active indefinitely or that their contents will not be altered.

SHARE AND TAKE ACTION

Volunteer at an animal shelter.
You can play and socialize with the cats or even foster a kitten!

Offer to pet sit for a neighbor.

Teach friends and family cat body language.
Know when it is okay to pet or play with a cat.

GLOSSARY

breed A group of animals developed from a common ancestor that are similar in looks and behavior.

bunting When a cat rubs its face against a person to mark them with its scent.

gland An organ in the body that makes chemicals or releases a substance or smell.

nocturnal Being active at night.

stubborn Determined and hard to convince to change.

vulnerable Able to be hurt or damaged.

INDEX

About the Author

M. K. Osborne is a children's writer and editor who lives in Minnesota. As an animal lover, Osborne enjoyed researching and writing about pet behavior and communication and hopes to inspire kids to pursue their own inquiries about pets.